Just Outside the Tunnel of Love

Flash Fiction
by Francine Witte

BLUE LIGHT PRESS ◆ 1ST WORLD PUBLISHING

1st WORLD
PUBLISHING

SAN FRANCISCO ◆ FAIRFIELD ◆ DELHI

Just Outside the Tunnel of Love

Copyright ©2023, Francine Witte

BLUE LIGHT PRESS
www.bluelightpress.com
bluelightpress@aol.com

1ST WORLD PUBLISHING
PO Box 2211
Fairfield, IA 52556
www.1stworldpublishing.com

BOOK & COVER DESIGN
Melanie Gendron
melaniegendron999@gmail.com

COVER ART
Journey by Carol Sessler

AUTHOR PHOTO
Mark Strodl

FIRST EDITION

ISBN: 978-1-4218-3527-3

Library of Congress Cataloging-in-Publication Data

For Mark

Acknowledgements

Grateful acknowledgement is made to the following publications in which these works, or earlier versions, previously appeared:

"Just Outside the Tunnel of Love," *X-Ray Lit; The Cake, The Smoke, The Moon Chapbook*

"Cab Ride," *Milk Candy Review; The Cake, The Smoke, The Moon Chapbook*

"1849," *Doorknobs and Bodypaint*

"Clean Magic," *F(r)iction Online*

"The Ice Cream Daughter," *Wigleaf*

"Even as Little," *Five South*

"Doorstep Baby," *Bending Genres*

"Even This Place Once Had a Mother," *Longleaf Review*

"When JJ Visits His Life," *Fictive Dream*

"1918," *Fictive Dream*

"Another Take on the Story," *Bending Genres*

"Home Shopping," *Unbroken Journal*

"In the Dark, Everything Looks Like Nothing," *Citron Review*

"Perfect," *MacQueen's Quinterly*

"Poor Josie," *Truffle*

"I Watch Daddy Tape Measure the Couch," *Southeast Review*

"Daddy Sits Us All at the Table," *Great Weather for Media*

"In the Woman's Head," *Cabinet of Heed*

"Thin Mints," *SmokeLong Quarterly*

"It Doesn't Rain Here Anymore," *Fictive Dream*

"All the Electric Things," *Ellipsis Zine*

Contents

Just Outside the Tunnel of Love

And Benny Jones telling me about Darlene. In other words, he pulled me through to unlove me.

Something about how love is a crispy pepper one minute, but then it goes wilty and soft. I told him I'm not a goddamn pepper and get to the goddamn point.

Problem is, I gave Benny Jones my heart too fast. My heart is a bristle I keep in my pocket and I can never wait to give it away.

Benny Jones sat in the boat in the Tunnel of Love, all squirm and tangle of words. *Friends*, he was saying, and *didn't mean to*.

Then he pointed to a pin's worth of light right there in front of us. "That's the future," he said. "It gets bigger and brighter the closer we get. All beautiful and warm." I told Benny to shut the hell up. If we're not a thing, we're not a thing, but don't go making a movie out of it.

When we did get outside the Tunnel of Love, into the future Benny Jones had promised would be warm and bright, I didn't see anything. I didn't feel anything. Just thought back to that summer at my grandma's house, when her old dog, Punch, got a fever and she was going to shoot him. How I stroked Punch's tan fur, telling him, *it's okay boy,* when I knew damn well it wasn't. My heart wriggling around in my pocket, even then, with no damn place for it to go.

Cab Ride

The meter starts, numbers twisting and ticking away, and it doesn't matter because numbers are a made-up thing, like love.

The city outside whirs by, men hammering buildings together, baby carriages, and store signs, all of it blurry and Monet. I'll put this painting in my head with the others.

The cab driver is 55 or 80, a hug of gray hair around his head. I don't think much about cab drivers. I figure they like it that way.

My mother, of course, is dying.

The cab driver drives past the hospital. "Wait," I tell him, "I said St. Elizabeth's."

"I know," he says, switching off the meter. "Let's go look at the river instead." I've heard of things like this. Kidnappings, hijackings.

One minute, my mother was asking if I wanted my eggs scrambled or fried.

The cab driver's eyes in the rearview. "Hospitals can wait a few minutes," he says. "My daughter," he continues, "she was only five."

When we get to the river, the slap of an autumn morning as we step out of the cab. All around us, the usual joggers, the seagulls climbing the sky.

"Those birds," he says, "they have this sense of direction. It's built into their wings."

We get back into the cab. We head to the hospital. I open the window and let in a whoosh of air, a sudden swoop underneath my arms.

1849

And the famine coming to a close. Thousands gone from potato death and the dumb, aimless wind wafting blight spores like music.

I was a girl, 16, watching from the window. My father, a human horseshoe bent over the crops. There had been nothing for days, and the last meal I shared was with Seamus Logan, 50 and breathstinking, fingers like old prunes. He ran the tailoring shop in town, and his wife had died mysterious. He'd let me come over for great meals of bacon and hunks of bread. His kisses were watery and foul, and I was trying my best to stay away.

I looked at my mother by the unlit, vacant stove. My brother, a tiny baby pulling at her teat. She stuck her thumb into his mouth as they rocked and rocked. How happy we'd be to all of us eat again.

My father came in, a basket of potatoes in his tan, ropey arms. "For me, and your mother," he said. "She's got to make milk for my only son."

My mistake was being a girl. Farm useless. I sat there, starving as they ate. Later, when they slept, I ran off for good to Seamus Logan.

Days went by, and Seamus told me my family was dead from the Cholera. "Blighted potatoes," he said. "The rot can sleep unseen for days."

And this was the start of the rest of my life. My future containing a given harvest of lovehunger and almost regret.

Clean Magic

1. Legless

He wakes, parch mouth and belly scratch. First thing he sees is Lily gone. Second thing, he is missing his legs.

They were his. Grown out of his hipholes, and how she took them without his waking is wonder enough. He always knew she would leave him, so far out of his reach. But he thought she would leave him his legs.

The drapes are pulled back. He likes to drift off sleepy to the moon. This time of morning, the sun has taken its place. Yellow and warm on the blanket. Right where his legs used to be.

And, oh yes, no blood. Nothing open where a severing might have happened. This was clean magic. Like Lily. He never knew where she came from. Just got caught one day in her hairflow and skinsilk – then poof!

But oh, how to live from here on? This is what. A glass of simple water. An ocean away. A bedroom walk, even a small one, is hard. One crawl, his hipbones bouncing over footprints. His arms, the arms that held Lily like a feathercloud, will have to be his legs, knuckling him to the kitchen, and then what of the sink?

His ache for Lily has to deaden now, no time for love or desire. He drops like an orange to the floor. He makes it across the carpet, but what about the door? The knob just inches too high. He looks around. No phone. Lily saw to that.

Nothing to do but wait. More clean magic, maybe Lily coming back. Meanwhile, the thirst for everything is draping the room like sunlight.

2. I Left a Man

Left him to hobble, bobble across the floor. I took his legs. I took his heart. That was the best of him. I took his legs so he couldn't come tracking after me. I took his heart because I could.

I'm an evil girl, some would say. Some others would say he's lucky. I could have taken his arms.

I left a man for all the men I didn't leave. For all the head-torn, heart-torn times and me rocking myself to sleep.

This time, I left a man who was kind, who stroked me gentle, sang me sweet lullabies. I was used to icy men, hearts of pure crystal. I didn't know how to take love. The last man I had was married, three children, left me clanging at his door.

After that, I fell into a hole of want. My life had been boiled away. I finally got up and searched for a magic fix. I paid a man five dollars for a rock.

I set it on the counter. It glowed like a woman in love. It grew my hair lush and dark. It pillowed up my lips.

First thing, I called the married man, said I had his stolen watch. He met me and fell mad in love.

I said, meet me later, pack a bag, and leave your squalling children. Leave your wife in a puddle of tears.

I watched his mouth, the mouth that had told me so many lies, say he'd be there with his life.

I waved his mouth right off him. And if he went to meet me later, I'll never, ever know.

3. What is it Like to be Magic,

but trapped, like I am, in a rock? I ought to be out in the world, greening the trees, or blushing the cheek of a bride.

Instead, I landed here. Sold for five bucks to a woman, burned with hurt, who uses me now for revenge.

I think of how I started, born in the heart of a star. Sprinkled across the nightsash. Soon after that, I started turning the seasons, lifting the sea, working always quickly and clean.

Now and then, something tricks me. This time, I entered a rock, mistaking its hardness for truth. My mouth is stopped up, gaglike; my voice is a muffled scream.

You would think I could wave myself out of here. Magic my own self free. But it has to pass in its own measured way, like time and dying and love.

The Ice Cream Daughter

For years, she ate nothing but ice cream. Bowls of it. Tubs. Her mother said words like "eating disorder" and "how will you live?" but the daughter just waved it away.

"The trick is," the daughter said, "to make the ice cream look like other things. Ice cream burgers, scrambled ice cream eggs…" For Thanksgiving she fashioned a turkey out of butter pecan. The other guests ooh-ed and ahh-ed, but the mother was still not convinced. How will she survive in the world when I'm gone?

Things only got worse when the daughter started dating a much older man. Ninety, if he was a day. The daughter was of age, by this time, but still the mother was worried. What about children? But the daughter, again, waved it away, saying that there were other things more important. His love of ice cream, for example. His toothlessness left him little choice, and so, he was easy to feed.

One Sunday, a few months after the daughter had sneaked off to marry, the mother went to visit. The fireplace mantel was filled with ice cream scoops and syrup jars, the way other people's were filled with family photographs. The husband sat in his armchair, quiet, the mother thought, so as to let the two women catch up.

The daughter made an ice cream roast. A lump of rocky road in a black speckled pan. The mother was eager to please her daughter, and so she had seconds, even thirds.

By dessert, the mother motioned to the husband. "I noticed," she said, "that he's been in his armchair the entire time. And he didn't eat anything at all. Tell me," the mother leaned in, "is everything okay?"

"Mother," the daughter said, "my husband was a very old man. He died soon after the wedding. Every day, I make a new husband out of ice cream. And every night I eat him for dessert. This makes me very happy," she said.

The mother watched as the daughter cut a slab of her husband's jacket and put it on a plate. The daughter *did* look happy. The mother took a deep, deep breath. A sigh really. She looked at her own long fingers, white as vanilla, and for the first time, she knew that her daughter would be all right.

Even as Little

As five years old, you would stand in the doorway that wasn't a doorway, just a spot in the park your father walked you to, told you *let's build a house right here that only the two of us know about and I can say something like Parkhouse in the middle of dinner, and you'll know exactly what I mean, and in this house I won't be out of another job and I won't have to ask your mother to make half for dinner, count out the bites of a pork chop to make it last longer, and we can slurp down buckets of soda if that's what we want,* and the trees would listen to all of this, shaking their October heads, leaf after leaf falling, all crispy and brown, and dead, and that's when another little girl, another father stop at the ice cream truck parked just across the way and the little girl won't have to eat it slow and slow trying to memorize the taste of chocolate with every tiny bite, and your father would see the look in your face, the haunt that would stay there forever, and say, *c'mon let's pick out some wood for our house, some magical tree that will know us even after we shave it into a wall,* and he'd take you by your little girl hand and you'd take one last look at the little girl across the road, her father handing her an ice cream cone, drippy and lush, and her not having to measure or memorize anything, about to take a bite.

Doorstep Baby

She marries. An expensive affair with live little people on top of an eight-foot cake. The music is a *jazzhiphopclassical* fusion combo whose leader is screwing the groom's mother. The groom is the last to arrive. When he does arrive, his breath is cover-up minty. She's never known it any other way.

• • •

She applies for Medicare. Her bones make noise these days. Third husband just left her. When she fills out the application, she is glad she didn't take his last name. His ass dent is still in the easy chair. That's easier to get rid of than a name.

• • •

Her father's sperm meets her mother's egg. This was not a well-thought-out meeting. No one set up chairs for this meeting or ordered snacks. This was a what's your sign and what the hell and I will never see you again kind of thing.

• • •

She is four. Doctor's office and her foster parents know nothing about her history. Doorstep baby, they tell the doctor. Doctor checks her eyes and nose and snaps the chart shut. Doorstep babies are strong, he says. Doorstep babies do fine.

• • •

She drives her second husband into a wall. Out for an afternoon, but they end up arguing about how she saw his mother out with a bandleader. No, the second husband says. That wasn't me. That was your third husband. She notices a loaf of bread moving on a nearby doorstep. She loses control of the car.

• • •

It's a calm day at the office. She is sitting across from Van. Van, her first husband, though she doesn't know it yet. He gives her a rose. To make up for the whole doorstep thing. She's about to ask how he knows when she gets trapped in the ocean(!) of his eyes.

• • •

Doorstep baby on a winter's night. Wrapped in a blue blanket. Note safety-pinned and scrawled. *Please take care of my baby. I was drunk and I never saw the father again.* Hungry old woman passing by thinks she is a loaf of bread, picks her up and tries to eat her. Drops her when she starts to squall. Almost gets run over by an angry woman driving into a wall.

• • •

When she dies, there is no funeral. No one was left. Not her parents, not her fosters, not the three husbands, not the doctor. She dies in a winter storm. The cold hitting her like a sperm meeting an egg, like a doctor snapping closed a chart, like an angry woman driving into a wall. Right there on the doorstep. A hungry old woman passing by.

Even This Place Once Had a Mother

Now, it's just a jut of car-bones and twisty tailpipes. Junkyard, Daddy calls it. We drive our ancient Honda there. The one where I was made, Mama once confessed before she died. The junkyard man counts out thirty dollars. *I guess we can sell this for parts,* he says. I think about my mama dying slowly, her heart unbeating, her liver, and then. I look at the ground under a pile of cars and wonder why someone didn't plant trees here instead. Daddy taps me on the shoulder, *Cab's here,* he says. Now that the car I was made in is gone, I wonder what will happen to me. I look out the back window of the cab, the doorless cars, the crunched-up fenders blending into one uncertain blur.

When JJ Visits His Life

He doesn't know it anymore. For some reason, his life is hunched over and wrinkled. JJ always figured someday there would be wrinkles. He even started a filler fund when he was twelve, stashing the apple money his mom was always sneaking into his pocket.

This isn't JJ's only life, of course. He had the one with Matilda, and then the one with Jane. And there's the work life, the race car life, the *I'll-put-it-all-on-eleven* life. But he thinks of this particular life now and again. JJ tells his life to sit down; I want to catch up.

"You left me at seventeen," his life says, "in search of who knows? Who cares?"

How come you're all wrinkled, JJ wants to know, if I left you at seventeen?

"I waited for you to come back," his life says, "after the flings. After the juts. You never did and somehow, I got older than you."

JJ, not one for physics or philosophy, says instead, I still have the apple money. I was saving it, but we can use it to make you feel better.

"I'm past that now," his life says, "I'm tired; it's best you leave. In fact, I was getting ready to die when you came in."

JJ, not one for confrontation, looks at this life he doesn't know anymore. Watches it curl up in exactly the same fetal pose JJ would get into those nights Mom and Dad fought like cats, or those other nights when some girl broke his teenaged heart.

JJ's life goes gauzy and ghosty right there in front of him, his voice little more than a tiny croak. "Hey, remember that night of Susy Benton's Sweet Sixteen, how her hair smelled like coconuts and we were afraid to breathe because it might make time move?" his life says, knowing the end is almost here.

"That was a pretty good night," JJ and his life both saying at once.

1918

Like every other night, Finkus creaks the splintery door, slips out of his only shirt and folds it over a chair. He smooths the coarse wool with his calloused hands, wets his thumb and rubs the spots. One, a splotch of mud from when he carried a lady's valise to a cab. Another one, grease from fixing a wheel on Goldman's pushcart.

Like every other night, Esther, his wife, looks as empty as bones, and fusses over a stew. A sliver of beef, but mostly the potatoes and carrots that Stein the grocer was going to throw away. Scrape the bad off of everything, he told her, and it will taste like new.

A little girl, she was, in Russia, and one night her father doesn't come home. Wandered into the wrong part of town and got kicked in the head by a horse. Soon after, a smuggled trip to America. Her mother only, and one suitcase between them. Later, she met Finkus, with his smile and his hair and his head of ideas. On her deathbed, Esther's mother called him a good man, "like your father," she said.

Like every other night, Finkus slumps onto the floor mattress they stuff with old rags. Too tired to eat. Too weighted down with the illness growing inside of him. The illness that will kick him flat like a horse's hoof.

Esther will sit alone at the table until the stew cools and wash the plate and put it back in the cupboard. Then, like every other night, Esther will pick up his shirt, and soak spots with hot water and use the kettle steam to smooth out the wrinkles before she sneaks it back over the chair.

And no sooner does she finish, Finkus grunts himself up and comes to the table. Hungry, he is for once. Tonight, won't be like every other night. Tonight will be the night he tells her about the illness. Isn't that what a wife is for, he thinks, to share?

He sits down in front of the still-warm plate. He notices his shirt in a way he never has. Cleaner, he thinks, and smoother, too. He looks at Esther for an answer. She looks at him for a smile. The clink of fork on the supper plate. She didn't ask for this, he thinks, and rather than tell her tonight about the illness, he swallows it down with the stew.

Another Take on the Story

"For sale: baby shoes, never worn."
– Ernest Hemingway

Maybe there had been a baby shower, and there was a registry with a pair of shoes on the list, but the baby's grandmother never checked the list, having spent the last few months in Europe, and she picked up the identical pair of shoes in a shop in Barcelona on one of her typical sprees.

Or maybe they were being sold, never used because the baby himself was such a charitable little chap and said (in baby talk, of course,) "Mama, I have everything I need. Please sell my unused, never worn shoes, and give the money to some unlucky baby who didn't have the good fortune to be born to you and Pop."

Or maybe still, the father's mistress snuck them into his briefcase, hoping the father would find them and realize what a generous soul she is, and he would leave his selfish wife like he was always saying he would.

Or maybe the father wasn't even sure in the first place if the kid was his after all. And who the hell cares if the little brat runs around shoeless, and he's just lucky not to live near a hillside.

But most likely, it's exactly what you thought, and the baby actually died.

Home Shopping

Late night, all alone. Amethyst twinkling from the TV set. The beautiful "o" of stones. I feel like an "o" myself, a zero, because 3 a.m. is when the world gets so quiet, you hear everything. The host is a piano of teeth and a candle of eyes. She says things like *special value, very rare*, and I'm thinking she doesn't mean me. No, she is talking about the necklace. Every stone faceted, perfect. She flickers it under the camera lights and the amethyst looks like nightstars which takes me back to my own summer nights, on a blanket with some boyfriend or other, the smell of sweetgrass and his ropey, teenaged neck. His hands damp, a tremble of lust and even the sky wasn't bigger than we were. I look back at the TV. I wonder if amethyst has a smell.

In the Dark, Everything Looks Like Nothing

1. At some point, my parents were young and happy. I have the photo to prove it. Black and white. Color of bones and midnight.

2. First day of teaching, all I do is hand out bus passes. I wonder if this is what my mother did on her first day as a teacher. Where's mine? a ninth grader wants to know. I can't find it, I say. Tell me your name again. He walks out in a huff.

3. My grandfather sits at a desk and talks on a telephone. I never said more than hello to him. Back then, grandfathers didn't speak to children. Whoever is on the phone isn't a child. I wonder if he ever spoke to my father.

4. The day my mother leaves, she waits till my father is at work. He works in the city and so she has time. My mother will not give me her new address. You are grown, she says. I'll call you when I can.

5. My father plays his clarinet. He holds it and looks at it like it's a baby. I must have looked like a clarinet once.

6. My last day of teaching, a student I don't know blows into my classroom. Tells me to watch myself after school. I mean it, bitch, he says and pushes me against the chalkboard. I have nothing to give him. Not even a scream.

7. My father is blowing out the candles. I have made him a party to soften the news that my mother is getting remarried. He is happy at this moment. Leaning forward, looking young again. Next week, my mother will also be young, dancing at her wedding like a bride.

8. We bury my father with his clarinet. He will play it in heaven, my cousin says. Everyone smiles and agrees. Except for my sister,

who never liked my parents. She says as soon as we're gone, the gravediggers will steal my father's clarinet.

9. My father also played the guitar. Strummed out sound instead of music. For a short time, he and my mother would sing together.

10. I leave my mother for the last time, certain she doesn't even know who I am. My mother probably used up all her words. I leave her in the room at the nursing home. It is early evening. She sits there in what is left of the light.

Perfect

In the low-light of morning, Mildred eases, teardrop, out of bed. She hasn't been much for sleeping, but last night was different, what with Harry visiting in a dream.

Everyone warned her. How death perfects a person. Her mother, pinching her arm at the funeral. "Look around," her mother whispered. "How many of his women are here?"

Mildred had known, of course. How could she not, what with Harry's constant preening and spice cologne. Mildred knew, but was love-prisoned, the bars of it metal and strong.

Egg yolk skittering now in the breakfast pan and Mildred can't forget the dream. What with Harry telling her to meet him by the river. On the high rock ledge where they had that first summersweet picnic. The jab and snag of the rocks and the two of them going naked and in love.

In the dream, Harry tells her his death is lonely. What with her still alive, able to eat and sleep and breathe.

She had thought of this herself, of course. What with day and day and day blinking its stupid pain at her. She had thought of wrist-slit and pill-swallow, but there was something always stopping her, what with fear kicking in, one last hope kicking in.

In the dream, Harry is perfect. His other women hidden from his face. His tongue gone empty of lies. And the dream itself, what with its broken nature, turning Harry to a bird to a river to a rock.

Mildred finishes her breakfast. It would be easy to go to the river, she thinks. Take the cobbled path up to the ledge. Fall teardrop into the river.

But, by now, the sun is full. Late morning when the truth scorches itself into her eyes. Harry will never be better than he was last night in the dream. Will never love her more than that.

Later that night, when Mildred goes to bed, she knows that Harry will be waiting there for her, longing for her, wanting her, and so she slips perfect into sleep.

Poor Josie

Has nothing. So, it's time to sell her house.

But not in one piece, thinks Poor Josie. That way, I can adjust.

She looks out her window one final time. This is it, old friend, she says. That night a man carts it off, all panes and glass of it. Nothing left but a hole in the wall and poor Josie scolding the moon.

Next morning, the door. Poor Josie hoisting it off of its hinges. Giving the doorknob one last kiss, tracing the grain in the wood. I'll miss you, she says to the door, a man hefting it up on his back, loading it into his truck. And Poor Josie scolding the wind.

And then all of the furniture, piece by piece. Poor Josie cursing her need to sit down, her need to sleep in a bed. At supper, and the cupboard empty of dishes, she curses her need to eat.

But the last of it, the worst of it is when Poor Josie sells the floor from under her feet. Board by board, it goes until there's nothing to stand on, and the dirt underneath the house too dirty, after all.

Josie, poor no more, but still, she has nothing, floating now in the houseless air like a stupid balloon.

I Watch Daddy Tape Measure the Couch

Because the gambling has got him again. Gambling is a dog that wants to eat Daddy bit by bit.

Last month, I watched him measure the TV set. Next day, it was gone, and Daddy telling us it was bad anyway for our eyes.

This has been going on for a while now. I thought Mother leaving him snake eyes would have changed him up, but no. Just made him rub his hands together. Like he was a camper and his hands could start a fire.

And that fire is burning him alive. I remember when I was a kid. Daddy and me on our nightly walks. The candy store with its lottery scratch-offs. Only two dollars. A soft blow on the fire. A soft stroke on the doggie's nose.

Now we live, just us two, in the third apartment down from the house he lost. Nothing much left. By tomorrow, not even a couch.

I try to sleep on my bed of bunched-up newspapers. I wake up dreaming of growling dogs, of matches striking like small tornadoes. I open the bedroom door to get Daddy. To get him to make it all stop.

But there, in the leftover light through the living room window, I see Daddy walking toward me. Tape measure in his hand.

Daddy Sits Us All at the Table

And tries to tell us about life. He starts with an orange. My mother had put a bunch of them in a bowl, all nice and hilly, before she left us for good. Now they were nothing but brown little stones.

"You see this orange," he says anyway. "It started out juicy and full of hope."

"Excuse me," my soon-dead brother, Billy, says. "How can an orange be filled with hope?" This was a fair question, but I suspect it's the kind that will eventually get him killed.

Daddy shrugs and says, "okay, let me try this with a fish." So he pulls one out of the cookie jar. We are smacked silly with the stink. It is gouged with rot and we are glad to finally be addressing it.

"Are you going to slice off its belly?" my Aunt Noma wants to know. "I'll gladly eat it with my lunch."

"Can't you see how spoiled it is?" Daddy almost says.

He turns around for a knife and Noma slips it in her purse. "If you give a dead thing purpose," she winks at us, "it's sort of still alive."

When Daddy turns back and sees the fish missing, along with Aunt Noma, he tries another way.

He walks us over to the nursery, the secret room we don't talk about. Where my brother, Baby X, died after only one week.

"This is what you need to know about life," he points to the crib I only saw once, and that was when it was empty. Either before or after Baby X.

Not during. Never during.

Daddy goes on to tell us how life is a garden. You water it. You run a hose. You think of what the seeds will grow into. You try to forget that death is also a seed.

Split

The day is slowing to a shiver now, slowing and blacking into night and that's when your father comes home, hole in his soul, and says things like *supper* and *bitch*, and your mother slams back *you're late, you're late.* And you, you are standing there, not knowing which way to turn, and the anger that was floating like daydust on the sunlight air springs up and gathers and plants itself in that hole in your father's soul, just digs and digs and your father is bare now, little more than a pair of hands lunging towards your mother who is broken her own self and is saying things like *I don't love you anyway,* and *if you only knew, if you only knew.* And you're watching all this, being pulled and pulled like you're taffy or a jump rope because you're still a kid, and you want to go to your happy place, a beautiful beach, where at any time you can walk into the ocean, go back to your fish self, the swimming sperm that crossed your mother's insides, that split second that you were about to become you. And the only trembling was coming from love and desire and if someone were to ask you at that moment, which one of your parents you needed more, you wouldn't have to choose.

In the Woman's Head

She is holding the cat; the cat is all she has in the gone-ness of love. Another man was clapped off the stage and went on to something other in his life. The woman has time now. She is too sad to work. She is makeup-free, stiletto-free. She can bake and eat and sleep too late. She has the cat to fill up her arms. She tempts the cat with a shatter of cat treats.

The cat is night-colored, eyes like white planets. After some time, the woman forgets to drop the treats, forgets to stroke the cat, but yanks the cat into her now fleshy arms. She squeezes the cat like a lemon, waiting for something to come out of the cat that the cat doesn't have.

She puts the cat down and tells the cat she's sorry. She isn't sorry, but says it anyway. The woman hasn't said real words in a very long time. She likes the sound of them, the full round shape of them. They float and drift in the air, the cat circling the floor underneath.

In the Cat's Head

He is holding the woman. He is in her arms, but he is in charge. The cat has cat-things to do, but the woman lures the cat into her arms with treats and the cat likes that. The woman seems to need something. The cat doesn't know exactly what.

The woman is beach-colored and empty. Her eyes liquid and puffed up like waterholes. The woman used to come and go and come and go, but doesn't anymore.

Before all this, there was a man. And when the man was there, the woman left the cat alone. Didn't try to hold the cat in her arms that were wiry and muscled. Didn't bother with treats, and words were tinny and constant.

Sometimes now, the woman forgets the treats, and the cat thinks that maybe this is what drove the man away. The cat would tell her that if he had words. He hasn't heard the woman's words in quite some time. So long a time, in fact, he isn't really sure what they are, and as the words start to fall to the floor, he circles and stalks the way he would if it were a bird about to fall from the sky, and him getting back to his own feral self.

Thin Mints

Girl Scout at the door, a box of *Thin Mints* in her hand. She is maybe 12 or so.

Bangs and peachy lip gloss. The purse against her hip is like the one my mother wore. Cobra skin and golden clasp.

• • •

My mother died eraser-like. One day there, then gone. After the funeral, my father built a mountain out of my mother's things, her purses and shoes. The mountain was shaped like my mother and slept next to him at night.

• • •

"We owe you, right? *Samoa's*, right?" I dig into my pocket. "Your father already paid me," the Girl Scout says. She points to the purse, "he also gave me this."

• • •

One night, after my mother died, I knocked and knocked at my father's door. Something about a leaky pipe. When he didn't answer, I creaked open the door. My father on the bed in a whiskey-sleep, his open hand on the purse.

• • •

"Your father home?" the Girl Scout asks, holding out the box of *Thin Mints*. "I brought him these."

• • •

It's a good thing I didn't want the purse myself. Wouldn't take it if you paid me.

• • •

When I was little, I thought the purse was magic. I had cut my finger and my mother said hush and pulled a blue band-aid from the purse's belly. The scent of cherry cough drops and lilac blending as she patched my tiny cut. When my mother died, I shook and shook the purse. Emptied it upside down. Nothing but lint balls and loose change. Not a scrap of magic.

• • •

My father is standing behind me now. "You said you'd like to try these," the Girl Scout says, offering my father the *Thin Mints*. "Oh, thank you," he says, ripping open the box. "This is good," he says. He holds up his hand, "wait here."

• • •

"You'd think we'd sell more *Samoas*," the Girl Scout is saying." Everyone says they like coconut, but I think they mean in their hand lotion. I tell her we like the *Samoas*. "Well, really, it was my mother," I say.

• • •

My father comes back with a pair of my mother's shoes. Taken right out of the mountain. "I'm trying to clear out a few things," he says, offering the shoes to the Girl Scout. "Maybe for your mama." She takes the purse off of her shoulder. "Thanks," she says, "my mom doesn't wear heels, and also, she says I have to give this back."

• • •

Later that night, much later, I creak open the door to my father's room. The mountain is gone, but everything is scattered all across the floor. Almost like someone took the room and shook it and shook it. My father, alone now, on the bed, staring upwards, as if hoping something might fall from the sky.

It Doesn't Rain Here Anymore

Hasn't rained for six months now. Dad likes it because he doesn't have to fix the hole in the roof. Mom likes it because no one is tracking in any mud. Whenever we watch the news, and the weatherbot comes on, Dad says this is *soooo depresso* and switches to another channel.

• • •

My brother, Dean, is big into astronomy. He has a telescope and it pokes straight up from the attic through the hole in the roof. Dean says there's another Earth and it's just like ours. He says there's a family that is kind of like us.

• • •

The weatherbot is really a woman. I call her a bot because I hate her. Mom hates her, too. We all know that we hate her because she looks just like the neighbor lady Dad was caught kissing that time. Her hair is fluffy and blonde in the same way, and there is something about her eyes. I'm sure Dad sees the resemblance but he pretends it's the lack of rain that bothers him when she comes on the screen.

• • •

One time, when it used to rain, Mom thought it might be nice to invite the neighbor lady over for dinner. I could hear Mom on the phone inviting her – "feel free to bring your children," Mom was saying, "I have two – 13 and 15." She was lying. I was never 13. I skipped it just like an elevator. Besides, 14 felt like the beginning of things. Boys, and makeup and well. . .life.

• • •

When the neighbor lady came over, it was pouring, and even though she was as careful as she could be, she still tracked mud into the house, and Mom was fussing behind her as they went into the living room. She sat on the couch and Mom took her shoes to dry near the stove. She was beautiful in a way my mother had no time for. Her face unlined, her nails, oval and glittered, the way I wanted to wear mine. She told us she had no kids, and she was alone in the house waiting for her husband to join her the next week. Mom said, "I hope you like roast beef." The neighbor smiled her perfecttooth smile, yes, she said, very much. My father came in just then and he looked at her in a way I'd never seen him look at anyone before, fixed and pinlike, the way I'd seen Dean get when he was looking up at planets.

• • •

Dean says the other Earth is flooding with rain. He says the father in our parallel family is packing his clothes, throwing everything into a duffel bag and leaving in a rowboat. He says the father is waving goodbye to the mother who is staying behind to make roast beef. Dean says the boy in the family is in their attic, looking through a telescope and he is staring directly at us. When I ask what the girl is doing, he looks again and says, "there is no girl."

• • •

When the hole in the roof happened, Dad said it was from a rock. I said maybe it was Tommy Metcalf from down the street. Dad said no, a kid couldn't throw a rock that hard. Mom said, maybe an airplane. Dad just looked up at the sky and said no, this is outer space we're talking about.

• • •

I start wearing eyeliner and scarlet lipstick I find in Mom's dressing table drawer. I'm 15 now, so it's okay. I think of the weatherbot and the lady next door and how I want to look like them. When I come down to breakfast, Mom says, I'm not 15, I'm 14, and that's still too young. I go back upstairs and I wonder how old you have to be to want people to see you.

• • •

Dad leaves one day and never comes back. Mom calls the police and goes next door to ask the neighbor lady if she's seen my father, but she's gone, too. Only her husband now, who is standing on the porch looking up at the sky. He turns to look at Mom and invites her in for coffee, but she hustles herself home and says we are a smaller family now and that's just that.

• • •

After Dad is gone a month, it starts to rain and rain and rain. Dean's telescope is only useful now to plug up the roof and keep the rain from coming in. Mom tells us not to watch TV because she doesn't want to see the weatherbot, but I sneak it anyway when Mom goes out to buy groceries. I like to see how the weatherbot wears her hair. I want to look at her eyes. One time when Dad didn't leave the room, he said this woman talks with her eyes. I wonder if that was because of her eyeliner or something else. Like maybe there was a star galaxy inside her.

• • •

The rain keeps on, and Mom hires a man to fix the roof. He pulls out the ruined telescope and says the hole was probably from pesty squirrels and there ain't no outer space anyhow. Mom is happy to have the roof all normal again and she invites the roofman to stay for dinner. She asks him if he likes roast beef. She goes upstairs and when she comes back down, her lips are suddenly scarlet.

• • •

At dinner, Dean tells the roofman about other Earth. The roofman leans back in his chair, Dad's chair, and says one Earth is plenty for him and can he please have more delicious roast beef. Mom smiles, her eyes lit up and pretty. On the roof, the rain a steady thrum almost like the sound of a thousand falling stars.

All the Electric Things

1973, the year Dad tries to give up electricity. The toaster, Mom's iron, Sissy's fancy blow dryer. Dad says we're soft, like butter. Mom says if we're butter, we'd stain the upholstery. Dad doesn't laugh. Sissy is upset about the blow dryer. She has class pictures the next day. Mom leans over and whispers she can use it when Dad isn't home.

We spend hours watching the TV without the TV on. Dad tells us stories about The Depression. Sissy says, "yeah, you were all depressed because you didn't have TV." Mom wants to smile but says, don't sass your father and lights the evening candles. "Isn't this nice now," Dad says. "All of us in this cozy glow? Don't we feel like pioneers?" Sissy points out the pioneers are dead and can she go to her room? She says she's going to send smoke signals to Chad, her new boyfriend, and stomps upstairs. Dad moves to get up to go after her. "Give her time," Mom says, pulling him back.

The next week, Sissy leaves us forever. Only 16, a runaway, but Mom doesn't call the cops. "No need to give her a record," she says, "besides, she'll miss us, the dinners, the evening chats." Then she tells Dad that we will need at least an hour a day of electricity. She needs to make sure Dad has presentable shirts. That she's tired of handwashing them in the bathtub and the wrinkles don't fade by themselves. Dad says it's all okay, his clothes look fine. Of course, Mom doesn't tell him about the washing machine she runs while he's out. "It's important," Dad says, "that we try to be better," and Mom agrees, but when Sissy sends us a postcard with only the word FREEDOM scrawled across the back, I swear I see a flick of electricity passing through my mother's eyes.

Moon Story

When she was little, she thought the moon was an egg. A round one. But an egg. Each month, when the moon was full, she would wait for it to crack open and drop its slimy yolk into the sky.

Then, as she grew, she thought the moon was a colorless eye staring and watching her every move. Every month, she would hide in her room, but stripes of white moon eye would peep through her window.

Then she was grown and met Bill, a morning person. They quickly got married and moved into a house, two kids and a dog. They all went to sleep by 7 p.m., and she forgot all about the moon.

Till one night the phone rings, hangs up, and rings some more. She goes to the window and stares at her long-lost moon. It is full and looks like the golf ball her husband must be using those mornings away from her.

She looks again and it turns into a numberless clock or, perhaps, a dinner plate.

Finally, she sees that the moon is the other woman's featureless face. No eyes or nose, just a hungry kiss mouth on the white moonscape. She wants to wake her husband to show him, show him the proof so she can leave him once and for all.

But instead, she gets little again, goes back to thinking the moon is an egg and waits for the cracks to appear.

My Father Takes Me to the Rodeo

And that's when I know what I want to be. Not the cowboy, flailing all spaghetti in the afternoon sun. But the horse bucking and shaking that small man off his back.

My father was out of work again. Third time this year. He explained it to me this way – Everyone's a liar.

When I asked my mother what he meant by that, she was on her last few weeks of him. Would leave him, leave *us* by the end of the month. "Ask him," was all she said.

My mother hated it here in West Gully. She still missed New York. Loved the knots of people, the sky you could only see in pieces.

Here, there was nothing *but* sky. My father moved us here and said the empty blue would give him a canvas to write on.

My father lost the first job because he stole money from the cash register. My mother and I knew he did it because he went out and bought himself a cowboy outfit, which he said was to fit in. And don't forget the boots with mother-of-pearl, a belt with a near-gold buckle. Course, he lost it all in a poker game. He lied about that, too.

So now, it's just me and my father, and he takes me to the rodeo even though he usually goes alone. He says the rodeo makes the kind of sense the rest of the world does not. "It's man against horse," he says. "Now, forget the man. The man is just a stupid fool, thinking he could tame something wild like that. But a horse. A horse will never call you a liar. He will just shake you the hell off his back. You show me a man who can do that."

It was something to see the truth coming out of my father's mouth, first time since forever. "I gotta be father and mother to you now," he said, the sun squinching up his eyes. "And I don't know how I'm gonna do."

We sat there the rest of the time really quiet. Sitting still in our seats while nearly everyone else jumped up and hollered. My father reached his hand over to mine, squeezed it gently. Every now and again the crowd around us cheering a cowboy being thrown to the ground.

Mom's Pumpkin Boyfriend

Carved out jack-o on the dresser. Mom first learned to do this last Halloween. Scooped the goo out of a pumpkin head when Dad was out on a drunk. Mom's own head a beehive of regret and wondering how on earth their marriage went so wrong.

Mom and Dad who must have been young, their faces turned upwards. And then years go by. Jobs, and then no jobs, Mom twinkling the neighbor's eye, Dad taking his first sip of gin.

So, tonight, it's one Halloween later, and Mom's pumpkin boyfriend is pretty much all she's got. Not the one from last year, of course. That one dried up months ago. But here's the thing about pumpkins – there is always another one, and also, they tend to stay put.

Dad is out, and I peek in to tell her I'm off to trick or treat even though I'm already too old. I see my mother sitting there, dressed in a negligee she has saved from forever. Air spiced up with Dad's cologne. On the dresser, her new pumpkin boyfriend, lit-up candle shining out of his eyeholes, a shot glass of gin up against his pulpy gashmouth, and Mom just watching, almost like she's waiting, to see if he's going to take a sip.

Bloom's Women

Bloom isn't much. Near 60, and like a bag of saggy potatoes. On top of that he smells. Like urine mixed with tobacco. But there are women, a number of them now, who find his odd smell sexy. Animal pheromones it says to their lonely vaginas.

There's the one he knocked up, and then the married one he wouldn't sleep with and the other married one he did. A few others besides all that. And, oh yeah, of course there is his wife.

This particular day, Bloom is on a quest for sunlight. Wants to warm his balding head. If he sits in the front yard, he knows what'll happen. Some passing-by woman will ask for directions, thinking Bloom is a safe, old coot. But when she approaches, leans in, that's when he gets too close to her nose.

At first, she will be disgusted by the stink. *Doesn't he wash?* she will wonder, backing away, convinced she was better off lost. But as she starts to leave, she will find herself unable to move.

That's when Bloom's broomstick of a wife will come out to chase off the love-struck female. "It's like having rats," the wife will say.

Bloom goes up to the roof. He has built a garden there. Lush and fragrant. Roses to blur his own odor. Sunlight strong, and here comes a bunch of bees waving ocean-like on the summer air. He thinks he'll be okay, but just then the Queen herself gets a whiff of Bloom. Flies too close on her way to the roses. Circles Bloom and lands on his shoulder.

Any minute now, his wife on the rooftop, newspaper in hand. Any minute now, a dead ball of bee-fuzz falling from his shoulder, another flattened female thudding to the ground.

Ten Winters

One. Moonbelly mother.

Two. I'm born. You still don't know who my father is, do you?

Three. We live upstairs from the sex landlord. How else to pay the rent?

Four, Five, Six. Each winter ripe with icicles. Snowballs thrown at my fatherless face.

Seven, Eight. Barely grown, I run off with a scummy old man. Maybe he can be my father.

Nine. I hear somewhere you are dying. Winter cold makes my eyes cry.

Ten. I put you to sleep forever in a splintery coffin. It wraps around you the way I could have/should have with my arms.

Tortellini Jones

Yes, she is named after the pasta.

Long version – it's what her parents ate at Tortellini's pre-conception dinner. There were also roses, but there already was an Aunt Rose.

Short version – by the time Tortellini was born, that story is all that is left of her father.

As she grows up, Tortellini turns beautiful. Her mother pales and dies, and when Tortellini is 18, she finds that she needs a home.

Tortellini will meet many men. Each one will look, or not look, like her father.

The men will find Tortellini delicious. Her buttery blonde hair, the blueberry of her eyes.

They will joke Tortellini. *If I warm you*, they will say, *will you soften to my touch?*

Tortellini has improved over the years. Now she just sneers.

Till Michael. She likes his normal name. Normal enough to balance hers. And she likes his non-jokey way. Besides, he smiles just like the photo father her mother kept next to the lamp.

Long version – Michael will ask her to marry, offer her a home. He will promise never to leave. Tortellini will think this is a good thing, but it's not. If Tortellini's father had stayed, there would be hidden-mistress years and tears behind her mother's bedroom door. Just like if Michael stays, there will be years of drinking and a right-arm hammer that finally comes out. Of course, this is only if Tortellini decides to get married.

Short version – she does.

Meta

I am watching myself. From way over here.

Look at me. Ridiculous. I'm nothing but a bad Rom Com. I would walk out if I could.

This one's name is Harry. Whatever. I'll have to forget it soon enough.

You take my mom, for example. She knew a good *over* when she saw it. First oof of another woman on my father's collar and she was off like *bam!* Left the baked beans boiling in a pot.

Harry is giving me flowers. Look at me, softening, my shoulders relaxing, my sniffer going numb. I am watching how I don't see him pull out his phone, texting texting. *Who is he texting?*

My mother told me not to look in the mirror. She said I wasn't pretty and she didn't want me telling this to myself every day. I asked her if I looked more like her or my father. You look like a heartache is all she said.

Soon after she said that, I saw myself in a store glass. It was only an outline, but enough to see that I didn't look like a heartache, even though I wasn't sure what that meant. I went inside the store. I bought my mother cigarettes like she asked and went home. I was going to tell her she was wrong about the heartache thing. I wanted to tell her. I would tell her. Someday I would watch myself tell her.

Even from here, I see how bored Harry is. I see myself sensing this and so I do what I always do. I ask and ask. He says nothing and nothing. I say I made blueberry pie. It's your favorite, right? Harry going stabby and pushing the pie around the plate and then *oops! Emergency. Gotta go*, he says. Harry sells paper goods. I wonder what a paper emergency would be. The me I am watching is wondering that. The me over here knows better.

My mom knew better. Not about my dad, though. Yes, she left him, left us, as soon as she saw the other woman on his collar but there was so much before. I saw it. Saw it when he drove me over to soccer practice and he leaned in too close to our coach, Miss Williams. And another time, and the time before that. My father never seeing how I was watching.

I watched my father die in the hospital. Car crash. Texting and took his eyes off the road. I called my mother to tell her. She had given me her number for emergencies. Your father's death, she said, is not an emergency.

Harry is gone now. I look at the space he left behind. I look at how I smell the flowers and stroke the flowers waiting for them to come alive and give me love. I watch how patient I can be. I look at those flowers even as I wash the dishes, scrub blueberry off the dessert plates. I walk by the hallway mirror, quick glance at the tracks of mascara on my cheeks. Then even closer. I am watching myself watching myself. I hear my mother in my head, *don't look, don't look*, she is saying. I turn away and grab a bottle of wine.

It's later that night and I watch myself sleeping. I look at the empty bottle of wine by my bed. I watch how I fell asleep in my clothes, my makeup still on. I look at how I'm clutching two of the carnations from the bouquet Harry gave me. I get this way about the things men give me, that their touch is still on them, that their breath is still on them and how that is the only part of them I will ever really have.

My mother was right; I do look like a heartache.

I crawl into the bed next to myself. I listen to the drunken whisper of my own sleep. I crawl back into myself through a dream. A simple one about mothers and flowers and fathers and blueberry. When I wake in the morning, I won't check my phone to see if Harry has called, but instead I will walk myself over to the mirror. I will look at myself now through my own eyes and when I start to shy from my reflection, I will turn my face forward, and hold it there if I have to in my own invisible hands.

Leftover Boys

Tommy and Bobby. Geometry class. Def Leppard T-shirts and gelled-up hair. They were like the fruit our mothers taught us to put back. Apples with bruises, berries gone squish. They weren't much, but then, neither were we. Fleshbelt under our crop tops and fake tattoos. Nobody looking, but we wanted more.

Old Mr. Barren, tap-tapping his chalk nub in front of the class. *Eyes forward,* he'd say. *What's the answer,* he'd say.

Kevin and Danny, they were the answer, though we didn't say. Back of the classroom. Flameless fire. Gorgeous and plum.

In the air all around us, triangles obtuse and leaning away from themselves. Same way we were pulled to the sound of leather squealing from their jackets. How we wanted to bury our faces there.

And then, Mr. Barren. His long gray suit next to us. Teacher smell, old paper and cafeteria milk. "Three times to the principal's office," he said. "Care to make it four?"

Everyone watching. Looking at us, the way they never did. We were movie star trouble. Danger dropping on us like a red-carpet spotlight. We looked at Kevin and Danny. Their eyes almost meeting ours.

After class, in the hallway, we leaned against the cool, green wall. Kevin and Danny breezing by us, scent of leather as they passed. We watched them getting smaller and smaller.

And Tommy and Bobby, trickling last out of the classroom. "That was bitchin'" one of them said. "Walk you to French class?" one of them said.

The two of them looking at us. The near empty hallway. Their arms going around us, their hands on our shoulders, moist and uncertain like skittery fish.

Different

My father tells me I'm different. He doesn't say how, or if different is bad. Just leaves the word twirling and swirling around like the time he flushed my not-dead goldfish down the toilet. He said he was teaching me a lesson. Wouldn't say what the lesson was or where the goldfish was going.

My father says get used to it. Again, doesn't say what *it* is. He likes being mysterious. Will disappear for days sometimes, or else he pretends he's James Bond. Tells my mother he wants his coffee shaken not stirred. Stuff like that.

My father tells me not to listen to boys. Not one of them can be trusted.

He says that because I'm different, boys will get me to do their homework. He says boys won't treat me well. That girls like me, who are different, will buy boys presents to get their attention. That boys will pretend they like me. Call me a good egg.

I look in the mirror for the egg part. I'm not yolky or runny or anything. When I tell this to my father, he says, well just be careful.

I *am* careful. And the night my father doesn't come home and it turns into forever, my mother is the one who turns egg. Cracked and shattered, sprawled like a pain-omelet on the couch.

That's when I know I'm different. Won't miss this man who tells me what I am but won't tell me. Leaves my mother and me swirling around and twirling around without giving us even a clue about where we are going.

Waiting Outside of the Friendly's

Me and Sasha, all dolled up like Barbie. Sasha all gooey with lust and black eyeliner. We were waiting for Ted, who would be pulling up in his Army-brother's rusty Mustang. We were going who-knows-where to do who-knows-what. It was getting dark, like forest-dark, like when all the pine trees hover over you and close up into night. "Maybe they aren't coming," I finally said. They, being Ted, for Sasha, and Larry for me. The two of them 19 and dangersexy. Me and Sasha still 16. Years later, I would run into Sasha at the very spot where the Friendly's used to be. I hadn't seen her since her oldest boy's funeral. That was the boy Ted had pumped into her that night so long ago. Her eyes were too puffy for eyeliner now. She asked if I'd heard that Larry drove himself drunk into a wall. I wanted to tell her I wasn't surprised given how he kept sucking on his beer can that night we all went out. How even though I saw him a few times after, he always seemed like he was headed into nothing, so why not a wall? Instead, I told her no I hadn't, and I tried not to notice the bruises like purple kisses all up her arm. "Too bad about the Friendly's," Sasha said, "I hate how things always change." And then she asked if I needed a ride. "Ted will be here any minute." And this time I knew for certain he would show up, even though I was wishing he wouldn't.

Potato Saga

I.

A lady falls in love with a potato. Why? Well, it's a handsome potato, so there is that. But when she fishes it out of the potato bag and hefts it in her hand, its eyes are facing up at her and God knows it's been a while since she's been looked at. She names the potato Harold, and etches a smile into its skin. She sets it in a cool, dry place to keep it fresh and longing for her. She strokes the curve of its forehead, the smooth bubble of it. She will buy it a beret, she thinks. She coos that she will be right back, shows up minutes later, negligee and sex perfume.

II.

It doesn't take long before the potato has had enough and rolls itself over to the open kitchen window. A potato's life, it reasons, is not very long and it's got to make the best of it. It rolls past trees and loamy fields; it gets a homesick ache for the heft of cool dirt on its back. The potato wonders if it ever had a mother. Do vegetables have mothers, it cries through his mouthpeel into the world that is sudden and huge around it. Nobody listens. The potato wonders if it's made a mistake.

III.

The potato chef asks the potato if it wants to be mashed or French fried. The potato chef doesn't usually pick up potatoes on the side of the road, but this one looked so…lost? And also, the potato chef is trying new things like calling it *road potato* or *found potato* on the menu. He certainly can't serve the potato baked, not with that weird-ass smile carved into its peel. The potato chef is really a line cook. His boss found him one day rolling around by the side of the road. Now the line cook likes to pretend that he is a potato chef, thinks of the mouth that this potato might end up in – the teeth gnash and savor juices breaking it down. Mashed or French fried – the first decision the line cook has made in months.

And if he is not mistaken, a very sad look in the potato's withery eyes, winning out over that potato's silly smile. The potato chef straightens up, picks up a knife – potato murder or mercy killing, the potato chef couldn't say for sure.

IV.

The lady is dressed up nice and fine – cloche and hat pin, et cetera. First time out in a week, the lonely week since Harold disappeared. The restaurant buzzes around her – clink and clatter and Frank Sinatra. *Good to treat yourself*, she thinks. Hunger is rumbling her stomach. The waiter takes her order. "Good choice, Madam, very special." So special in fact, that the line cook brings it to the table himself. The potato soup she ordered in Harold's honor. The line cook beams as she takes her first ferocious sip. "I'm so glad you like it, Madam," the line cook says. "This potato in this soup was no ordinary potato. Why do you know, it had a smile carved into its peel?"

May/December

May is, frankly, fed up. Yesterday was the six-month mark where her relationships usually die. Today is six months plus one.

She wants to end this, but can't break an old man's heart, so she breaks some eggs instead. Only this time she'll add something disgusting. Something that will curl his taste buds and force his tongue to say break-up words to her. She considers shoe polish, but that might make it murder.

December wasn't always an old man to her. Started as her father's best friend. Adventurer, took animal photos in Africa, had the whole Hemingway thing. Took her to places guys her age didn't, took her home and swirled his tongue inside her. Sometimes she would pretend she was a felled gazelle and he was a lion gnawing and gnawing. That sort of thing.

December hasn't been anywhere lately. Grown a little jowly, too. He stumbles into the kitchen. He has embraced the Hemingway part about drinking and his eyes are billowed and shot. He grabs her from behind as she's stirring the pan. The eggs are bubble and pop. He unties her bathrobe and slides his hands over her. She is falling, falling, felled. What is six months plus two she thinks and doesn't think anymore after that.

A Martini Walks Into a Bar

ate for work! The bartender yells and goes on rubbing circles into the hardened five o'clock counter. Outside the sun is the color of a smile. "I'll have a white wine," the martini says folding his glass stem onto the barstool. The bartender pours the wine and calls the martini an alcohol cannibal. The backroom of the bar, where the booths are and usually filled with tinkly love, is filled instead with the pleadings of an ugly man. He is asking his *Tinder* date why the ugly are not entitled to love. "Why is it," he is saying, "that we have the terrible luck of scraggled hair and bulbous nose. We are always scooping out a place in our hearts for one more hurt." The *Tinder* date has eyes that are the color of *not my problem* and says this conversation isn't working. The bartender tells the martini, "go do your job. I'll put some Ella on the jukebox." Too late. The martini passes the *Tinder* date who is heading for the bar. The martini jumps up on the table. He glides into the ugly man's mouth who takes a furious sip.

A Bartender Walks Into a Bar

He is hoping today will be better. Hoping those weird martini visions will stop. The sun outside is the color of his cheating wife, and he's been staring at it for answers. This staring has caused haloes and blurred retinas. He picks up a rag and circles the hardened wood. *Why do I have such terrible luck? Why do I have such terrible luck?* The bar stopped answering ages ago. Said something like this conversation isn't working and can I just go back to being inanimate? From the backroom of the bar, the tinkly bells of another heart getting shattered. The bartender puts Ella on the jukebox, hoping to drown it out. That's when the martini shows up and orders a white wine. The bartender hates himself for feeling a bit of relief. He tells the martini to lean forward so he can take a sip. The martini tastes like things that might have been, but aren't. The martini is the color of *dude, pull yourself together.* The bartender nods and tells the martini about the ugly man in the back and as long as you're here, go make yourself useful. "Before you go," the bartender says, "let me take another sip."

An Ugly Man Walks Into a Bar

First thing, he orders a martini as he heads to the back. The sun outside is the color of false hope. He gets to the booth and starts to think handsome thoughts. He brought a rose and chocolates for his *Tinder* date. *Maybe*, he thinks, *she will get all sugar-rushed and won't focus on my jaggy teeth and droopy ears.* He sits and waits for his martini. When his *Tinder* date arrives in her long-fingered, tornado-haired way, the ugly man is instantly enchanted, bewitched. Tinkly bells start to ring. She strokes a glass of wine that she says the bartender gave her when she entered. She says that is what it's like to be beautiful but of course he wouldn't know. That's when Ella pops up sudden in the air. The *Tinder* date brushes back the roses and candy, says this conversation isn't working, that his being so ugly is only making her even more beautiful. She leaves the table and heads to the bar, passing the martini who is making its way to the table. The martini is the color of a martini. The ugly man looks over at the bar and sees his *Tinder* date making out with the bartender. The ugly man tells the martini, "quick jump up on the table so I can drink the ugly off of me." Soon, the martini and the man both become more beautiful. Soon, they are singing along with the jukebox. Outside the sun is the color of an olive sinking in the sky. The ugly man takes another sip.

Not-Myrtle

Of all the things I could be doing tonight, I have chosen to fall in love with you, which is kind of like swimming bare-assed in the Everglades, alligator snap all around, trying to ignore that you just hit on my best friend, Tess, who I plainly saw you buying a dirty martini for and trying to stand out from the rest, what with Tess always being the beautiful one, and I'm lucky if I even get seen, how we can walk into a bar and me with my cat eyeliner and contour jawline and Tess in her I-didn't-have-time-to-change-after-work pantsuit, the kind that Hillary would wear, but somehow Tess fills it out in non-Hillary ways, what with her bump of hip and jut of boob, and even with Tess looking over at me as if to say I'm sorry I'm so fucking beautiful, and me wanting to say, you don't have to say you're beautiful, everyone can see it, and martinis are hurling themselves towards her even though she never asked, and she's all no thank you, no thank you, and this is my best friend Myrtle, even though that isn't my name, we use pretend names just in case, and it might as well really be Myrtle for all anyone even cares, and like I said, I could have been doing any number of things tonight, crossword puzzles or pulling pimento out of those olives because really, no red food, but here I am giving the universe one more try, and you look at me, with that After-Tess in your eyes that I have seen so many times I could put it on a postage stamp, and I see you are just a little less alligator than most, because I also saw how you had to throw back a shot or two before you could walk over to Tess in the first place, her with her pearl-necklace smile and nothing but no thank you no thank you for your trouble, and how she turned you towards me and said, this is my friend, Myrtle, who is really good at crosswords and eye makeup and when I finally saw your eyes looking straight at me, I could see a half a dozen alligator bites already in them, and I'm thinking that maybe it might be okay to try to put together all our chewed-up parts, you and me, and see if they form one pretty good thing.

One Day, Lucy Cannot Find Her Head

Normally, she would try to think where she left it. But now she cannot.

This is not completely unexpected.

Men don't like smart women, her mother had warned.

Men only want your body, her father had warned.

Women don't look good in hats, her sister had warned.

Meanwhile the head part of Lucy is right there in the kitchen. Lucy had been in the middle of a cookie recipe. The head was filled with ingredient words like whisk and nutmeg, and Lucy was getting overwhelmed. The kitchen was hot and Lucy left the babbling head on the counter while she walked into the other room to cool off.

After a while, the head was sweat on its forehead, hoarse from calling and calling to earless Lucy. Lucy, who was now bumping into everything as she wandered the apartment like a stupid *Roomba.*

Finally, the head gives up, deciding, like only a head can do, that it is the main part of Lucy, after all. That's where all the memories are, the appointments, and the knowledge of long division. The head takes a deep sigh breath. Happy now, it closes its eyes.

Meanwhile, the rest of Lucy, the arms and legs and heart of her land inevitably in the kitchen. If this part of Lucy could think, it would reason that it is the most important part what with all the getting to places and digestion and such.

But since it can't, since it's no more now than headless Lucy, it lies its bruised and tired self down on the kitchen linoleum, wrapping its arms around itself, its chest rising into the humid air.

In the Pool at the Lala Motel

In the deep end.

Where Charley told me to wait. Holding a mai tai, maybe, something with a bit of sass. Our honeymoon, it was.

The night before the wedding and Charley pacing the floor. I called my Florida mother, who said *jitters* and *sorry to miss*.

The wedding itself. Charley, the last to arrive. Whiskey on his tuxedo breath. His best man nudging him towards me like a beer.

And the honeymoon. One of those pay-by-the-hour places just out of town. Charley mixed up the mai tai from a gas station packet. Ginger ale from a vending machine.

It was noon, and Charley still hadn't touched me. *Saving himself*, is what he had said. I always wondered why he never wanted to kiss me or why he even wanted to get married. It's not like he lost a bet.

The pool, a skim of leaves and small insects. Most of them dead, but some trying to make it to the edge. "Guess no one swims here much," Charley winked, when he saw it, when he walked me down the steps, colder, then colder, then cold.

"Let's walk in up to our necks," Charley said, taking my hand towards the deep part, where probably no other person had been. "Wait here," he said, "I want to get my camera."

Every so often, a stray couple wandered out through the motel door and dipped a toe in the pool. Every so often, a fly made it close to the rim, maybe three breaths left, his wings soggy and useless, now, too heavy even for flight.

Owen Will Tell You

That his name begins with a zero and not the letter O. He will insist that you need to know this. It explains me, he will say.

People are always correcting him. Go ask your mother, they will laugh. He will breathe deep and tell them he is motherless. Found on a doorstep, like he was. I began with a zero, and the name just followed. This is where most people walk away.

Right now, Owen with a zero is at a job interview. The thirtieth this month. Everything will go fine until Owen brings up the story of his name.

But this time is different. The interviewer's name is Sally, whose name is spelled with a dollar sign and not the letter S. Her mother was a prostitute, her father a ten-dollar trick. She says that people assume she's a gold digger and how it has nearly ruined her life.

When Owen hears this, he goes instantly squishy with love. Sally hires him on the spot, both for the job and as her husband.

Years from now, their children will have no name issues. And if Owen has anything to say about it, they won't even have any names.

Eve to Me

It's crowded at the CVS, plink of toothbrushes dropping into baskets, Phil Collins music in the air. There is a bank of scanner machines at the checkout. They stopped letting humans do that here. I am waiting in line, when out of nowhere, Eve shows up. Eve from The Bible. Eve from the slithery snake.

I have a box of hair dye for my graying roots, hot pink polish for my nails. I'm trying new things since I found my husband's second phone in the bottom of his gym bag.

A woman ahead of me is yelling at one of the scanners, calling it a stupid, useless turd and can she please speak to the manager.

Eve is fig leaf and no makeup and she pulls me aside and says, "look, I didn't have any choices but you do. For me, there were no other fish, and if we did have *Tinder*, it would have been Adam, Adam, and more Adam."

Eve stops to look at the scanners. She doesn't seem very interested in the woman who is now pounding a fist on the screen that seems cool and unresponsive, as if she's not even there. Instead, Eve asks me what happened to the registers, the one with receipts that used to curl out of them, long and sinuous.

My husband doesn't look at me anymore. *I* don't look at me anymore. When I tell this to Eve, she says that no one looks at anyone anymore, not really. Too many of us, and not at all what was intended. Humans just doubled and tripled and grew like a virus that not even another virus can kill off.

I ask her what made her listen to a snake of all things. A snake is not like a husband that wraps itself around you like you are a tree, squeezes the very breath out of you, changes the color of your hair and nails. I ask her what Adam was doing while she was in the garden, and I suggest that she might have not been talking to a snake if Adam would have noticed her once in a while.

The scanner woman is being escorted out by Security, the manager pointing the way, telling the woman never to return. Eve looks troubled as if she's been triggered by the throwing-outness of all of this. She says, "look I gotta go. Good luck with your husband."

I move up to the scanner now. I wave the box of hair dye over the sensor, its red eye blinking, blinking. I look at the screen to make sure it sees it. Sees *me*. Some little sign that I exist. That I'm not just standing in a line of women all through history who felt invisible. A line that stretches all the way from Eve to me. Stacked one behind the other, each one wearing a touch more eyeliner, a shade deeper of lipstick than the one that came before.

Speaking Harry

When Harry says hello, he means for now. He means let's see how the evening goes. He means he might or might not have something else come up and he will have to leave.

When Harry says I brought you flowers he means this is still not an engagement ring. It will never be an engagement ring, so don't even ask.

It's a good thing I speak Harry. There are subtleties that only a trained ear can pick up.

When Harry says, I'll put these flowers in a vase, he means these flowers will die in a few days, so don't get attached. Notice I didn't bring a houseplant. Notice I didn't plant you a tree.

When Harry says let's order in, he means don't go getting all wifey on me. Don't cook me fancy-schmancy chicken while you wear your frilly little apron that would look pretty good during sex.

I haven't always been fluent in Harry. I still had the language of others bumping around in my brain. When I was eight and Tommy from across the street said, let's play tag, he meant let's end up behind the bushes and pull down our underwear.

I had to learn to speak Harry as if I had landed from another planet and Harry was the first human I had ever seen. Even though many of the things he said sounded exactly like things other men had said, they all had just enough nuance to make it seem different.

When Harry says that takeout was great, he means what's next? What's next?

What's next is sex, of course, and when Harry says the sex was amazing, he means please notice I still didn't say I love you. He means we did some damn fine things to one another. We were skit-skatting like Frank and Ella. We should be an exhibit in a sex museum.

When Harry says, be back in a minute, I have to pee, that's just what he means.

When Harry says, I'll bring a toothbrush next time so I can stay over, he means I want you to be confused. I want you to turn and turn this over in your head. He means, I still haven't told you I love you. He means his language doesn't even have a word for love.

When Harry says goodbye, I'll call you, he means maybe and whenever. He means it like something you say when you've just had scorcher sex with someone and it's just sooooo awkward getting to the door. He means of course his language has a word for love, every language has a word for love. It's just not one you'd understand.

Hashtags and Handles

@16andprego

#boyssuck

@aloneandprego

#TWINS!

#thankgodformom

#motherssuck

@sheltermom

@alonewithtwins

#theycryallthetime

#babiessuck

#canthandleboth

@worriedmom

@brokemom

@crazymom

#lefttheminsupermarket

@freeagain

#freedomsucks

#hearthemcrying

#stillhearthemcrying

RADIO to KNOLL (a wordle story)

RADIO

Again, I wake up to Adult Contempo. Taylor Swift eakling into my dreams. Why can't I grow up, I say out loud to my husband, who is already in the shower, steady thrush of water. He doesn't need an alarm. Love, he says, is what jets him out of bed. I want to think he means love of his morning coffee. We pre-set the *Keurig* the night before, and it waits for him all beany and steamy and eyepop. I want to think he means love of the crisp, ironed shirt he will put on, how the starchy smell makes everything seem new again. I want to think that this is what he means by love. I know that's not what he means.

OPINE

I'm up now. My husband sits across from me at the breakfast table. The morning paper spread out in front of him. He is eating the frozen waffles he likes so much. Jelly, no butter. He says he likes a burst of fruit. He opines on the paper. Stocks and murders, murders and stocks. He never mentions his secret girlfriend which is really all I want to know about. I want him to opine on the length of her hair, the color. Is there a burst of anything when he kisses her? Does touching her breast make him feel new like an ironed shirt makes him feel new?

KNOTS

Eddie, who is not my husband, has been teaching me to tie knots. Says it's a useful and undertaught skill. He says, you wait. One day when you least expect it, you will want to tie something and make sure it's tight as it can be. Eddie, who is not my husband, always smells like musk and sex he didn't shower off. I would breathe him all day if I could.

KNOCK

My husband has taken to knocking on the door whenever he enters a room. Even if the door is open. He does that thing where he says knock, knock while rapping on the door jamb. Knock, knock, he will say like I don't see his starchy, lying, fruit-filled self standing there waiting for me to acknowledge. Like he maybe wants to reboot me like a computer and start over where he and I meet for the first time and he would have to make sure I know he's there before he shatters me into a thousand pieces.

KNOWN

It's not exactly known where and when my husband ran off with his girlfriend. I know there's a half-jar of jelly leftover, so it's been since then. The where is another story. Eddie, who is not my husband, is sitting now at the foot of the bed. He says if I had known how to tie a knot, I could have secured my husband, maybe to an armchair, maybe to the breakfast table. He says people always make the same mistake about other people – that they will be exactly where you left them. Eddie, who is not my husband, still smells of sex he didn't shower off. He is naked right there, right then. He crawls towards me with a silky scarf between his teeth.

KNOLL

Definition – a hillock, a mound. Most likely green and grassy. Most likely peaceful. Most likely a really good metaphor for love if you lean that sort of way. To make everything a metaphor. Like years pushed all together and it only adds up to a mound instead of the mountain you were counting on. A wide-open field with a small bump of soil, and there you are knowing all the knots in the goddam world with nothing tall enough or sturdy enough to tie anything to.

Just Another Road Trip Story

Throw in a woman. Throw in a man. Throw in a brokedown Chevy. Throw in a body in the trunk.

Throw in a gas station. Bramble and brush. Hopper pumps and rattlesnake shiver.

Throw in the hot armpit sun.

Throw in the woman's husband who, of course, is in the trunk.

Throw in the way you eyed the *Door Dash* guy. No, that's another story.

Throw in Arizona. A road trip story is always Arizona.

Desert and plump of dune in the background. The man, the woman, the husband in the trunk pulling into the gas station. Throw in a lonely pop machine where only a quarter will roll out a Coke as crisp and cold as movie Christmas.

Throw in the gas station attendant about to open the trunk. *I'm gonna check the spare for air*, he probably says.

Throw in the way your husband doesn't look at you anymore. Not with anything close to desire. Throw in how you kinda, sorta understand the woman in the road trip story and whatever she did to put her husband in the trunk.

Throw in the man throwing his meat fist on the trunk, *thanks anyhow, old man, we just need gas*. Throw in the smell of rotting corpse working into the Arizona air.

Throw in how your husband goes corpse when you tell him your life is a desert and his love would be like water.

Throw in the gas station attendant going fisheye with suspicion.

Throw in how he sidles inside and rings up the sheriff. Throw in a shootout at the end of the road.

Throw in your refrigerator, dune in the background.

Throw in no one there to check if anything needs air.

Throw in you just sitting there with no idea how this story will end.

Waterfall

Not a honeymoon, but an early marriage trip and they are standing by the edge of Niagara Falls. That spot where the river ends and hurls itself into mist and spin. She is gripped by the dark shelf underneath the inches of water and how inviting it looks. If she were anything but human, maybe. If she were a barrel, say, or even a fish. She watches the water curling over like a question: *What have I done? What have I done?* She asks herself again that night back at the hotel. After the spill of sex with this husband she doesn't love. She lies there after, river-still.

• • •

Years later, she is shopping in one of those stores that replaced another store. She is two husbands later, but nothing much has changed. She picks up a bottle of cheap water. The faint slosh inside of it reminds her of something. Kind of.

• • •

Drench and cool and all of that, but really so much more. Her youngest, the second marriage baby, *the let's-try-to-save-this-marriage* baby, is now 22. She watches her dance in a small waterfall near their vacation home. Part of the divorce settlement after the husband took off in the night with the grocery woman, the one who handed out samples of water. The one he said wasn't that pretty.

• • •

It's funny, isn't it, how calm a river can seem? A water hollow, a rut in the earth and it fills up with rain or snow melt from the mountains. The twist of fish that keep swimming and swimming, a whole world going on underneath. It all keeps moving and moving and then . . .

• • •

Her third and final husband likes to go fishing. All day long, the slimy worms, the sinking damp. And worst of all, the stink.

Can't even wash it off anymore. It was something she couldn't have seen in his profile pic, her older daughter urging her on. "C'mon," she had said. "Dad's moved on and so should you." Later, she tells herself okay, she is a river and moving on is the only way to get anywhere. The next day she and the older daughter make a list of what she wants in a husband. Fish stink is not on the list.

• • •

She takes an old-lady trip to Niagara Falls. A bus ride with lots of Gwendolyns and Ruths. This is what she was always afraid of, bowls of gray hair and let's be sure to eat early. They break into groups of three at the restaurant. Talk about their dead husbands and how none of them saw it coming. They order olives in their salads because you have to have some fun at our age. They go back to see the Falls at night, lit up rainbow-style. She looks for the spot where the river turns into the Falls. Even with the colored lights, it's harder to see than in daytime. She wonders if the fish swimming directly into this spot can see it from upstream. She wishes for a moment that she could warn them.

Sequel

It's not important what happened before. The past with its burnt-out lightbulbs, its crumble of petals and such.

• • •

The way he was waving goodbye that last time and how it all seemed over. But wait it really wasn't. So, he calls one night, like everyone said he would. Coffee blah, I'm sorry, blah blah, I still love you blah blah blah blah blah.

• • •

TBH there was no before story. Not one that was written down.

• • •

The mother and the father go back to the house they raised their children in. The one the bank took when the father lost his dad job at the downtown company where he went each day with his coffee and paper and winked at the secretaries clackity clack. When he waved goodbye to his life, to his dream job. Today, he waits until the family living there goes on vacation. He tells his wife, shhh, stay in the car. He goes over and lights up his newspaper, waits till it flames up and places it under a pile of leaves by the porch.

• • •

A woman watches a reunion show she loved as a kid. How half the time is spent on how they look now, how wrong they grew into their new bodies, how unexpected given how cute they were. She looks at a photo of herself, her husband, her baby. She switches to the rerun channel and watches an episode of the original show. She looks at her photo and says, "don't."

• • •

To the store and back again. To the store and back again. To the store and back again. Then one day, you're gone.

• • •

A prequel note just for contrast. Before the girl grows up and marries Mr. Wrong, the one who will beat her senseless and she won't be able to leave, and will have to teach the kids to go play in their room when Daddy's car drives up, before all that, there is the look on her own mother's face at 10 p.m., ruined pot roast in the oven. Father working late again, but everyone knows it's another woman, and Mother saying what can you do? *What can you do?*

• • •

The buds of April. No surprise, but after such a long winter. Snow choking the streets like every other year, streams of car exhaust, warm it up, warm it up, and then out of nowhere, spring.

• • •

The thing of it is, we are still living our childhood. Whatever we do, we learned to do it then. We are simply *Superman 2, Godfather 2*. Good movies. Maybe better than the first.

• • •

This time, we want the reruns to turn out different. One hundred times, but maybe this time Ross doesn't cheat on Rachel. Maybe this time, Lucy tells Ethel this isn't a good idea. The same thing you have seen a hundred times, and a hundred times you are still wondering what will happen. *What will happen?*

Terror at the Top of the World

"They're coming," Jean-Louis says. "It's louder than yesterday."

His father is stirring their supper. Beans in a can he pounded open with a stone.

"Maybe," Jean-Louis says, "we should go norther."

"There is no norther," his father says. He pours some of the beans into his shoe and gives the can to Jean-Louis.

"I'm not even cold anymore," Jean-Louis says. "And look, the ice is turning back to water."

"Good," his father says. "We will need that to drink."

"I can smell the smoke from all the fires." Jean-Louis says. "I couldn't smell them yesterday."

"That's why we have to practice not breathing," his father says. "Soon all the air will be gone."

He takes a deep breath, his chest rising up with it.

"It's good we got here first," Jean-Louis says, eating the last of the beans. "It's good the others didn't believe us."

The air explodes out of his father's mouth. His father squints, looking south and then souther. "They believe us now."

"There will be thousands of them," Jean-Louis says. "Millions. They will take all our water. Take all our air."

"Don't be afraid," his father says. "The weaker ones will die off. Some won't even make it."

"We're gonna make it, right? Jean-Louis says.

"Come on," his father says. "Practice with me. Try not to smell the smoke."

The two of them standing straight as poles. Filling their chests with dimming air.

Near, then nearer, the sound of thudboots on the icecrack. The sound of backpack babies crying, then whimpering, then not.

About the Author

Francine Witte's flash fiction has been published in numerous journals and the anthologies *Flash Fiction Funny* (Blue Light Press,) *New Micro: Exceptionally Short Fiction* (W.W. Norton,) and *Flash Fiction America* (W.W. Norton.) as well as *Best Microfiction* and *Best Small Fictions.*She is the author of three flash fiction chapbooks, *Cold June,* (Ropewalk Press) winner of the 2010 Thomas Wilhelmus Award, *The Wind Twirls Everything* (Musclehead Press,) and *The Cake, The Smoke, The Moon,* (ELJ Editions.) Her novella-in-flash *The Way of The Wind* (Ad Hoc Press,) was cited as a highly recommended selection in the Bath Flash Fiction Award. Her poetry chapbooks include two first-prize winners, *First Rain* (Pecan Grove Press,) and *Not All Fires Burn the Same* (Slipstream Press.) She is the author of two full-length poetry collections, *Café Crazy,* and *The Theory of Flesh,* (both from Kelsay Press.) She is editor of *Flash Boulevard*, published by George Wallace. She is the flash fiction editor of *South Florida Poetry Journal.* She is a former high school teacher. She lives in Manhattan, NYC with her husband, Mark Larsen.

Personal Acknowledgement

Thank you to my husband, Mark Larsen, for his endless and tireless support of my writing, and for being my first reader.

Thank you to my darling sister, Lori Drucker, who watches me from heaven now.

Many thanks to all of the journals in which these were published, to the wonderful editors and staff.

Eternal gratitude to the workshop leaders who gave me the prompts and encouragement to write many of these stories. Among them, Meg Pokrass, Kathy Fish, Nancy Stohlman, Tommy Dean, Meg Tuite, Robert Vaughan, Len Kuntz, Jonathan Cardew, and Sarah Freligh.

Thank you to Carol Sessler for her beautiful painting, "Journey," which appears on the cover.

Thank you to Mark Strodl for the author photo.

Thank you to the Twitter and Facebook communities for providing the support of my stories and an opportunity to share my work.

Thank you, Sherrie Flick, Michael Martone, and Michelle Ross for your generous blurbs.

Thank you to the Flash Monsters who heard many of these stories in their infant stages, Leonora Desar, Lucien Desar, Al Kratz, April Bradley, Anne Weisgerber, Pat Foran, Paul Beckman, and Patricia Bidar.

Thank you to George Wallace for his editorial help and his support and friendship and for trusting me with *Flash Boulevard*.

Thank you to Lenny DellaRocca and Michael Mackin O'Meara for trusting me as flash fiction editor for *South Florida Poetry Journal*.

Thank you, Diane Frank and Melanie Gendron and to everyone at Blue Light Press for your beautiful books and for your support and hard work. I am honored to be on your roster.

Thank you, Beth Gilstrap, for your excellent proofreading.

And lastly, thank you to all my friends in the flash world and everyone who has taken the time to read my work. It means more to me than you will ever know.